POEMS FROM HEAVEN

Volume Two

POEMS FROM HEAVEN

Volume Two

JIM KINTNER

©2019 Jim Kintner

All rights reserved. No part of this book may be used or reproduced in any manner whatsoever without the prior written consent of the author. All art presented in this book is free of royalties.

ISBN: 978-0-0578-52333-0

ISBN-10: 0-578-52333-7

This book is dedicated

to Marylynn, A.J., Lindsey,

Grace, Mac & Addie

for their years of

love and support

● ● ●

TABLE OF CONTENTS

POEMS

1. At the Table ----------------------------------- 11
2. By the Sea -------------------------------------- 13
3. From the Cup---------------------------------- 15
4. Imagine-- 17
5. Signs of Wonder ------------------------------ 19
6. The Lord Cometh-----------------------------21
7. The Apostle Paul ----------------------------- 23
8. Just for Us-------------------------------------- 25
9. Jesus's Awakening---------------------------- 27
10. The Celebration of Christmas---------------- 29
11. The Man from Nazareth---------------------- 31
12. At the Temple --------------------------------33
13. Hail Mary-- 35
14. Easter Blessings------------------------------- 37
15. The Touch of Jesus --------------------------- 39
16. May God Be with You ------------------------ 41
17. The Providence of the Lord------------------ 43
18. God's Way--------------------------------------- 45
19. God's Speed------------------------------------ 47
20. Lord of All--------------------------------------- 49
21. The Wonder of it All ------------------------- 51
22. In God We Trust ------------------------------ 53
23. From the Beginning-------------------------- 55
24. Greater Than Great ------------------------- 57
25. A Higher Power ------------------------------ 59
26. The Lord's Plan------------------------------- 61
27. The Road to Righteousness-------------------- 63
28. The Giver of Life----------------------------- 65
29. A Child of God ------------------------------- 67

Introduction

● ● ●

The second volume of Poem from Heaven Poems is published at the request from friends and family. In the last year the inspiration to write the poems in this book came from scripture, sermons, bible study and hymns. I'm still amazed that the inspiration and content came to me with the help of The Lord. The poems are chaptered into eleven distinct and different subject matters. The Life of Christ, God, Faith and Redemption, and Healing Through Faith are several of the chapters in the poem book. As with the poems in my first book, "Poems from Heaven", I shared the poems and was encouraged by the members of my church, "St. John's Lutheran Church" in Palm Desert, California to publish this second book of Christian poems. I thank them for their support and encouragement. I am truly blessed to have written this second volume of Poems from Heaven. I truly hope that you enjoy them as much as
I enjoyed writing the.

Jim Kintner
Indio, California
September, 2019

30.	Salvation	69
31.	By the Grace of God	71
32.	Finding Grace	73
33.	Getting Closer to God	75
34.	Never Walk Alone	77
35.	A New Life in Christ	79
36.	Thankful for Christ	81
37.	It's God's Call	83
38.	In Times of Trouble	85
39.	Healing the Wounded Soul	87
40.	Praying for Relief	89
41.	Beyond My Control	91
42.	With the Lord by Your Side	93
43.	Saved by An Angel	95
44.	Jesus at the Wheel	97
45.	A Day in Heaven	99
46.	Time for Prayer	101
47.	Meditations of the Heart	103
48.	The Sermon	105
49.	Welcome to Worship	107
50.	Finding Your Soul	109

THE LIFE OF CHRIST

"Now as they were eating, Jesus took bread, and "after blessing it broke it and gave it to the disciples, and said, "Take, eat, this is my body". And he took a cup, and when he had given thanks, he gave it to them, saying, "Drink of it, all of you, for this is my blood of the covenant, which is poured out for many for many for the forgiveness of sins"

Matthew 26:26-28

AT THE TABLE

The Last Supper, the only meal of its kind,
Jesus telling his Disciples, what was on his mind.
The words of institution, offered by Jesus,
Bread and wine, remembrance offered, by the one that freed us.

The Disciples in wonder, did not know what was coming next,
The statements made to Jesus, later becoming biblical text.
So great the dinner, Christ's last meal,
Thereafter, before the Lord, everyone would kneel.

God's plan for his son, was about to unfold,
The saga historically called, "The Greatest Story Ever Told".
Jesus telling those he held so dear, please have no fear,
I came to earth to die, and after death to reappear.

No one could believe, the predictive words he had spoken,
The Messiah, was soon to be arrested, tortured and broken,
The significance of being at the table,
Disciples tasked to spread the word, telling the world of Jesus's fable.

We now are at communion, and celebrate that night,
His body and blood, given, in remembrance, honoring his birth right.
As he departed to Heaven, he gave his last adieu,
His final words to his Disciples, "Peace Be with You".

THE LIFE OF CHRIST

We have no more than five loaves and two fish – unless we are to go and buy for all these people. For there were about five thousand men. And he said to his disciples, "Have them sit down in groups of about fifty each." And they did so, and he had them all sit down. And taking the five loaves and the two fish, he looked up to heaven and said a blessing over them. Then he broke the loaves and gave them to the disciples to set before the crowd. And they all ate and were satisfied."

Luke 10:13-17

BY THE SEA

Each time I go to the shore,
I think of Jesus at Galilee, walking ashore.
So gracefully he walked across the waves,
Knowing that he was the only one that saves.

How was it possible, that he could float across the sea,
The miracle caused them to say, "You're the one to make us eternally free!".
Thereafter, the Lord calmed them down,
He said, "Relax, I won't let you down or drown!"

The next miracle, blew them away,
Bread and fish for 5,000, there was nothing more they could say.
The Messiah just took it all in stride,
The Disciples overwhelmed, now numb, they just went along for the ride.

Nothing that happened then, could be explained,
When they told others, they were called insane.
Their faith and devotion as Disciples, carried them through,
The Lord in control of His destiny, the miracles seen just a preview.

THE LIFE OF CHRIST

"Lord Jesus on the night when he was betrayed took bread, and when he had given thanks, he broke it, and said, "This is my body, which is for you. Do this in remembrance of me". In the same way also he took the cup, after supper, saying, "This cup is the new covenant in my blood. Do this, as often as you drink it, in remembrance of me."

Corinthians 11:23

FROM THE CUP

The source of life, from a cup,
Christ's blood given, a religious wake up.
Dedicating yourself to Jesus Christ,
Honoring the life that was sacrificed.

As a child, a small cup in hand, designed not to tip,
Small hands learning to pray, trying to take a sip.
Sunday school, a child's first communion,
Joining the holy trinity, a forever union.

Baptized by water, from a cup,
Told about heaven, the reason to always looking up.
The path to salvation, communion each week,
Attending church, and learning to pray, faith to seek.

Success arises from work, no doubt,
But faith in Christ is really what it's all about.
Honoring and remembering him, bread and wine,
Touching Christ in remembrance, so divine.

THE LIFE OF CHRIST

"Therefore, God has highly exalted him and bestowed on him the name that is above every name so that at the name of Jesus every knee should bow, in heaven and on earth and under the earth, and every tongue confess that Jesus Christ is Lord, to the glory of God the father."

Philippians 2:9-11

IMAGINE

Reading bible stories, about Christ,
His power and glory so great, yet God had him sacrificed.
I'm dreaming and imagining, being one of His own,
Walking with Him in Judea, never feeling alone,

Listening to His prophecies, but not understanding,
He was healing the sick, performing miracles, but there was no grandstanding.
So common His manner, his love having so much power,
Yet he calmly would say, "wait for my final hour".

His preaching on the mount, revelations, good news for thousands to hear,
Telling God's plan for all, making the world's future, perfectly clear.
Most uncertain, His prophecy so new, all listening in total disbelief,
Unaware that Jesus was their savior, giving them an eternity of relief.

At the shore, watching Jesus walk on water,
The mysteries of God, working magic underwater,
Five thousand followers, waiting to be fed,
Fish and bread for everyone, his power now widespread.

Imagining being present, being with Jesus Our Lord,
Bread and wine at the Last Supper, a heavenly award.
Death, resurrection, Christ's last forty days,
Christ's story so surreal, it left the World totally amazed.

THE LIFE OF CHRIST

Then Herod summoned the wise men secretly and ascertained from them what time the star had appeared. And he sent them to Bethlehem, saying, "Go and search diligently for the child, and when you have found him, bring me word, that I too may come and worship him."

Matthew 2:7-8

SIGNS OF WONDER

Wise men traveling by star light,
Magi's bearing gifts, Bethlehem in sight.
The prophecy of a Messiah, driving them on,
God's son's arrival eminent, starting the New Testament marathon.

The prophecies of John the Baptist, soon to be,
Sins of the world, soon forgiven for free.
The inn keeper's foresight, to send Joseph and Mary to the stable,
No quarters available, part of God's timetable.

The countdown starts for the coming of Christ,
Centuries in building, the drama set, ending in sacrifice.
Angels gathering, to announce the birth,
Heaven's messenger, ready to be sent to earth.

As the world slept, things were about to change,
God's plan for man, bringing a new heavenly exchange.
Signs of wonder, unfolding on a silent night,
Christ's birth, the beginning, starting at first light.

THE LIFE OF CHRIST

"God so loved the world that he gave his Only Son, and whoever believes in him should not perish but have eternal life."

John 3:16

THE LORD COMETH

The Lord's arrival on earth, prophecy fulfilled,
Peace, hope and joy, God's promise, the world so thrilled.
A Messiah child, born to the Virgin Mary,
A day so glorious, thereafter the day would start with "Merry".

God's timetable uncertain, the Lord's arrival, left the world with years of doubt,
Many heard of Christ's birth, rumors circulated and lies began to sprout.
What was God's plan for his blessed son?
Would he intervene? Heresy and sinners rampant! Miracles needed to be done.

Uncertain times following Christ's birth,
Roman legions persecuting all, thereafter crisis on earth.
The high Jewish Council, denouncing the Lord,
Great commotion arose, Pontius Pilate ready to use the sword.

To resolve the madness, God sent Jesus to bring peace,
Two decades passed, then God's powers were released,
Miracles and preaching came, the future was thereafter secured,
God's plan for man, salvation reassured.

THE LIFE OF CHRIST

Paul, a servant of Christ Jesus "called to be an apostle, set apart for the gospel of God."

Romans 1:1

THE APOSTLE PAUL

The conflict between gentiles and Jews,
Driven by hatred and mistrust, Ephesian news.
Paul sent to make the peace,
His weapon "Faith", his goal, anger to release.

The Lord had given him special powers,
His strength and message, turning Jewish rabbis' hour by hour.
Finding a way, to bring Peace to the land,
Using the Lord's Gospel, always directed by his guiding hand.

A biblical "Mission Impossible", in the ancient world,
Amid turmoil and chaos, Christ's battle flags unfurled.
The Lord's love prevailed, making all fighting to cease,
The reconciliation historic, the praise of the Lord thereafter released.

The Apostle Paul, committed as a disciple beyond reason,
The Jewish High Council, there after charging him with treason.
The miracle of faith, continued after Paul's death,
It brought Peace to the world, the Word, Christian shibboleth.

THE LIFE OF CHRIST

In God was life and the life was the light of men. The light shines in the darkness, and the darkness has not overcome it. There was a man sent by God, whose name was John. He came as a 'witness, to bear witness about the light, that all might believe through him.

John 1:4-6

JUST FOR US

The Book of John, a biblical story,
Chronicling Christ's life, true religious glory.
Each book and verse, a precious writing,
John's words, holy gospel, worth reciting.

From the Garden, to the Temple, to the Sea,
The parables so legendary, they foretold, what was to be.
So humbling and simple, the story so great,
Honoring Christ for his gifts, his death was his fate.

Our personal journey through time,
A test of our conviction, heaven or hell, an absolute paradigm.
With the Lord's gift of eternal life,
Our faith and acceptance, paired together like a drummer and fife.

"Just for Us", the Lord died and was resurrected,
Our Christian beliefs, are now always protected.
Holy Communion, bread and wine, we take to honor the Lord,
We give thanks for our blessing, Jesus so adored.

THE LIFE OF CHRIST

"I am the resurrection and the life. Whoever believes in me, though he die, yet shall he live, and everyone who lives and believes in me shall never die."

John 11:25-26

JESUS'S AWAKENING

God sent Jesus to Earth to be born,
The birth happening on a glorious morn.
No one understood, what would come next,
God promising peace, patience urged at His behest.

Banished to Egypt, to avoid Herod's wraith,
The young Jesus learned Jewish teachings, to understand His path.
Herod's persecution, hate, insurrection and more,
Taught the young Jesus, change was in store.

Praying to His father for guidance, as time marched on,
Jesus's awakening, God's Plan, brought a new dawn.
Love and understanding, the tools He used,
Fighting Romans, doubters and Jews, with God's good news.

Jesus grew in wisdom, with God's help He understood.
Quiet and reserved, no miracles, even though He could.
Slowly but surely, the crowds saw His light,
Through His message and sacrifice, all understood God's might.

As the Old Testament prophecy foretold,
Jesus hit the road, Preaching God's words, released man's heavy load.
Through Jesus's awakening, God brought hope to all,
Preventing global damnation, and humanity's fall.

THE LIFE OF CHRIST

"Today in the town of David a Savior has been born to you; he is the Messiah the Lord"

Luke 2:11

THE CELEBRATION OF CHRISTMAS

The birth of Christ, a day like no other,
Celebrated by millions, God's gift, from the womb of His mother.
A day to Honor Christ, as Our Savior,
Yet Christmas is so complex, it affects our behavior.

Buying Christmas trees, gifts and mistletoe,
The joy of the season tugs us to and fro.
From the prayers and hymns at Christmas worship,
To family gift time in the morning, honoring our capitalistic entrepreneurship.

Confusing at best, yet, it's the holiday season,
Family, friends and others, gather to watch football, needing no reason.
I started thinking about the start of another year,
Wondering what successes and setbacks, might next appear.

Nostalgia and Auld Lang Syne, bring tears to our eyes,
We celebrate a new baby girl's first Christmas, in spite of her cries.
Santa Claus never gets old, nor do his elves,
Decorations and lights aplenty, now on the house, not on the shelves.

Food and drink, meals that never end,
Family conversations, new revelations and political positions to defend.
It's the Celebration of Christmas, shared in so many ways,
Bringing Peace, Hope and Joy, during the Holidays

THE LIFE OF CHRIST

"People of Israel, listened to this Jesus of Nazareth was a man accredited by God to you by miracles, wonders and signs, which God did among you through him, as you yourselves know."

Acts 2:2

THE MAN FROM NAZARETH

History is filled with greats from the past,
Only one stands out, with adoration that will forever last.
Nazareth, located in the Middle East,
A small town, famous because of Jesus,
visitors will increase.

Over two thousand years ago,
It wasn't a place, where anyone wanted to go.
Dusty dirt roads, led to many a humble clay house,
So desolate, deserted, no sign of a cat or mouse.

Out of this place, God's son, made his way,
Neither Herod nor Pilate, could change the script of His play.
From birth to death, and resurrection next,
Jesus kept the Roman Empire, quite perplexed.

Who was this man, from another time and place?
Talking of God, as His father, leaving without a trace.
A mystery, the source of His miracle work,
Quoted as saying, "I'm part of an angelic network".

His death on the cross, paid the ultimate price,
Passage for us to the holy trinity, and Heaven's paradise.
From a village, that Jesus called home,
The man from Nazareth, greater than all the Emperors of Rome.

THE LIFE OF CHRIST

"After three days they found him in the temple courts, sitting among the teachers, listening to them and asking them questions. Everyone who heard him was amazed at his understanding and his answers."

Luke 2:46-47

AT THE TEMPLE

A dream, at the temple, with Jesus present,
Seeing the son of God and having sins to repent.
Hearing his words, a message from God,
Feeling insignificant, Jesus's radiance infinitely broad.

My faith now so great, that the dream feels real
The scene described in the scriptures, stamped with a holy seal.
The message is peace, hope and love,
Jesus with a scroll in hand, guided by God's hand above.

The wonder of this dream, ever life changing,
Just now so humbled, the imagery so emotionally rearranging.
The ability now to feel the Lord,
His presence within, bonded in faith, a heavenly accord.

Now back to reality, my dream has ended,
It's just another day, more time in a life extended.
The biggest blessing from my spiritual trip,
I keep the Lord close, engaged in a personal courtship.

THE LIFE OF CHRIST

When the angel Gabriel was sent to Mary by the Father, he greeted her, "Hail, full of grace; the Lord is with you."

Luke 1:28

HAIL MARY

A special prayer honoring the Mother of Christ,
Thanking her for her son, and his gift to us, being sacrificed.
The greatest Mother of all time, was so blessed,
Chosen mother of the Messiah, at God's request.

In the annals of history, she is the only one chosen for this role,
Making and delivering our Savior, with her mind, body and soul.
The holy mother, so perfect, an angel of the Lord, Absolutely the only
one ever given Devine Conception, awarded an evangelical accord.

From the stable in Bethlehem, to Christ's last day on earth,
Mother Mary was ever present, loving him with all her worth.
Sharing his suffering, death and ascension,
Assured to join him in Heaven, in our Lord God's dimension.

To this day, her contribution to Christianity, is an untold story,
In Reverence to the Lord, we have focused solely on Christ's glory.
Anyone selected by God, should be called a saint,
As we pray and recite our, Hail Marys", it is with devotion and love,
and with the need to acquaint.

THE LIFE OF CHRIST

"With great power the apostles continued to testify to the resurrection of Lord Jesus. and God's grace was so powerfully at work in them all."

Acts 3:33

EASTER BLESSINGS

Easter is a special time to praise the Lord,
Not a day for a parade, strutting around, wearing a uniform and sword.
Bonnets and bunnies, not the best theme of the day,
Meditation and prayer the way, to bring faith into play.

Easter eggs aplenty, colored, in a rainbow display,
Hidden everywhere possible, to initiate child's play.
This practice once became so popular,
 it seemed to make light of the day,
 Some not wanting to be serious, disregarded what the Pastor had to say.

As time has passed, Easter now more sacred,
God's message across, all now knowing where not to tread.
A glorious sunrise, at the early worship service,
Honoring our Savior, singing hymns, no disservice.

The day so special, Easter Lilies on display,
Reverence, faith, and prayers abound, it's Lent, the Lord has paved the way.
An Amazing experience, celebrating Jesus's rise from the dead,
Alleluia, Thankful that the Lord rose, his flock saved, eternal life ahead.

THE LIFE OF CHRIST

"She was freed from her suffering in her body, but Jesus wanted to touch her soul as well. The woman had snuck up behind Jesus in the anonymous fashion. As his power flowed into her body, Jesus knew something was going on. He stopped in the crowd having "realized that power had gone out from him."

Mark 5:30

THE TOUCH OF JESUS

The Bible stories, legendary and true,
The "Touch of Jesus", miraculous, as his fame grew.
The power of God, in just one mortal man,
Jesus's healing touch, part of God's plan.

Upon His arrival in a town, immediately, a crowd would form,
Excited to see the Messiah and seeing a miracle only he could perform.
A suffering woman, rushed to touch His robe,
Suffering for twelve years, she was ready to explode.

Jesus's touch, cured in an instant, her suffering stopped,
When confronted by Jesus, she begged for mercy, to His feet she dropped,
Jesus saying, "Your faith has cured your ills",
Arise and live woman, I have no more thrills.

Into the house, a young girl feared dead,
Jesus grabbing her hand, assuring her, no fear to dread.
She arose from the bed, and walked around,
The family in disbelief, His miracle of life, she had found.

The "Touch of Jesus" still with us today,
Now invisible, but it still works anyway.
Those so lucky, to feel the touch of His hand,
They bless Him as Lord, praising Him, right where they stand.

GOD

"Be strong and courageous. Do not be afraid or terrified because of them, for the LORD your God goes with you; he will never leave you nor forsake you."

-Deuteronomy 31:6

MAY GOD BE WITH YOU

As man searched the world, to parts unknown,
In the jungle, up the mountain and into the desert, all a danger zone,
There were Words of trust and faith, that all knew,
"May God Be with You", hoping to return, counting on the words to be true.

For hundreds of years, God's protection was requested,
God's love for man, was often tested.
Only a true believer, could be given relief,
With life ending peril ever present, safe passage based solely on belief.

Yet these words are still used today,
Astronauts into space, exploring, trying to find a way.
Or ocean explorers, going to the darkest deep,
Looking for answers, trying to find creatures that creep.

The wonder of the Lord, that protects us all,
Willing to save anyone taking risk, from a close call.
May each and every one of us truly believe,
So, God may protect us, and give a life ending reprieve.

GOD

"And my god shall supply all your need according to His riches in glory by Christ Jesus."

Philippians 4:19

THE PROVIDENCE OF THE LORD

Throughout the annals of history of civilized man,
The "Providence of God" requested, upon it, success would stand.
Whether it was exploring new lands,
Or building a new city, using thousands of hands.

The job's success or failure, always a nation's test,
It would often rest upon the Lord, and the task being blessed.
Was it fate? Was it all just being gloriously uplifted? Probably just man being heavenly gifted.

Historians have recorded, every great deed,
Always with the church's support, for all to heed.
It was blasphemy to say otherwise,
Life ending for some, they were not the smart guys.

Therefore, every bridge, dam or superhighway,
All were, done successfully, "Blessed", all would say.
There was nothing positive, to take a different position.
Always better to have a "christening" and make it a project condition.

So, if you're doing anything new, or out of your zone,
Ask for the Lord's help, approval and grace, before you pick up the phone.
Truly the Lord is always near, so be kind and humble,
Ask his permission through prayer, no need to fail and fumble.

GOD

"And we know that for those who love God all things work together for good, for those who are called according to his purpose."

Romans 8:28

GOD'S WAY

When something is perfect, it's not luck,
Just look up, think of the Lord, don't be thunderstruck.
God's powers are so great,
When he uses them, it's called fate.

He taught Houdini, some of his magic moves,
And sharpened Secretariat's famous hooves.
Michelangelo was taught to paint,
He worked hard making Joan of Arc, a beloved saint.

He took Einstein, on a ride through space,
And gave Usain Bolt, fleet feet to race.
He was in the boat with Washington, crossing the Delaware,
And with Lewis and Clark, when they were lost in nowhere.

He has shaped the world, and brought man along,
Never taking the credit, as He's never wrong.
So omnipotent and mighty, He's the only one,
That when light was needed, He created the sun.

God's way is the reason we pray,
Honoring His son, Jesus, in the prayers we say.
For those that believe in His power and might,
We ask for His help, on our knees at night.

GOD

"Fear not, for I am with you; be not dismayed, for I am your God; I will strengthen you. I will help you. I will uphold you with my righteous right hand."

Isaiah 41:10

GOD'S SPEED

The speedometer of your car, doesn't apply,
To the phrase, "God's Speed", no matter how hard you try.
For over three hundred years,
The words said to travelers, who had real fears.

During this time, the coach and buggy, the only mode of travel,
Danger on the road, many a travel plan would unravel.
Highwaymen, robbers, thieves, the journey's cost,
Nothing taken for granted, life and limb, perhaps lost,

Family and friends, sending loved ones on their way,
Wishing them, "God's Speed", the Lord's protection in the fray.
It's a mystery who God protects at any given time,
The extra blessing given perhaps, ensuring the trip would turn out fine.

The wonder of it all, that Our Lord is always watching over us,
Protecting, nurturing and perfecting, and thus,
History and Tradition, have taught us some special lessons,
"God's Speed", truly one of God's most used blessings.

GOD

"The Plans of the LORD stand firm forever, the purposes of his heart through all generations."

Psalm 33:11

LORD OF ALL

The prophecy of Jesus, the coming Messiah,
Brought fear to the Jewish elders, calling him a pariah.
A man so with God, he was sent to change the world,
A global panacea, but no flags unfurled.

Died and resurrected, like no other,
His powers so great, yet unknown to his mother.
As God's son, He became Lord of all,
The King of Kings, answering only to God's call.

Loved for His gift of life eternal above,
Adored by all Christians, given His glory and love.
No man that has ever lived, that had His power,
Only the Lord Almighty, the man for every hour.

It's hypocrisy, to not rank God above all,
All mortals, just human beings, just answer to God's call.
The wonder of His power, controlling life and death,
Once God' Grace is granted, effective just after one's last breath.

GOD

"Blessed be the Lord God, the God of Israel, who alone works wonders. And blessed be his glorious name forever; and may the whole earth be filled with His glory. Amen and Amen.

Psalm 72:18-19

THE WONDER OF IT ALL

For millions of years, earth has been,
Not by pure luck, God, the answer therein.
Some would say evolution brought it all,
With Nature's symmetry so perfect, I say that one's a tough call.

Millions and millions of galaxies in the sky,
Too many to count, why even try.
Learned astronomers say it's a must,
Religious leaders say, "the Lord made it all, believe and trust".

Just think of the wonder of it all,
Mother Nature vs. God, both having great wherewithal.
It's Darwin vs. the Bible, a historic match,
With God's powers present, that one is a true mismatch.

After thousands of years, there's still doubters,
Denying God's wonder, many ignorant shouters.
Embracing the Lord, a lifetime spiritual gift,
His wonder so great, pre-arranged, a believer's heavenly lift.

GOD

"Trust in the LORD with all your heart and lean not on your own understanding; in all your ways submit to him, and he will make your paths straight."

Proverbs 3:5-6

IN GOD WE TRUST

Our country was founded on these words of God,
Our nation's faith, Lord based, all patriots have trod,
For over two hundred fifty years,
Our success as a nation aided by God, citizens never felt their fears.

President after President, professing "In God We Trust",
We must never forget, that faith is something we can't adjust.
The future of the nation, resting on God's grace,
The surge of humanity today, now looking for some morality to embrace.

The confusion created by the Devil's work,
Causing so many to go berserk,
The only solution to this mess,
Go to church, as all have sins to confess.

Prayer in the schools, stopped by a new law,
Started a progressive reform, that has become a real flaw.
Our "Pledge of Allegiance", still says "One Nation Under God",
Any argument against, a moral fraud.

So, let's get everyone on the same page,
Which is, "The Lord is King", our number one sage.
So, when we say, "In God We Trust",
We pledge ourselves, and say, "Heaven is a Must".

GOD

"I will instruct you and teach you in the way you should go; I will counsel you with my eye upon you."

Psalm 32:8

FROM THE BEGINNING

At birth, the glory of life revealed,
The Lord, creator, maker, all to yield.
His wonder, each person unique,
Urging each one of us, faith to seek.

His voice with us, each day,
His message to heed, the church is the way.
At Sunday school, lessons in Christ learned,
His reward, confidence and faith rightfully earned.

As the years go by, His presence, the foundation of success.
Never worry about the future, no need to guess.
Like money in the bank, grace is given to you, Jesus Christ,
Our Lord Savior, will carry you through.

"From the Beginning", a life to live,
Eternal life guaranteed, nothing to give,
From your heart and soul, the journey pure and good,
A Christians life filled with faith in Christ, never to be misunderstood.

GOD

"The LORD has established his throne in the heavens, and his kingdom rules over-all.

Psalm 103:19

GREATER THAN GREAT

Time is measured, in millions of years,
Crowd appreciation in the number of cheers.
Some things, difficult to measure,
The number of jewels, in the King's Treasure.

In the two thousand years, since Christ was born,
Measuring his greatness, has left some forlorn.
Water to wine, healing the sick,
Just God's Power, so miraculous, not a cheap trick.

Rising from the dead, after three days,
Greater than great, in so many ways.
We're humbled by the wonder of our Lord,
So complex and unimaginable, His story to record.

In all the things that have ever occurred,
Christ's greatness is absolutely absurd.
So great that the mind can't comprehend,
Our Savior, His gift, a promise to the end.

GOD

"For I know the plans I have for you." declares the LORD, "plans to prosper you and not to harm you, plans to give your hope and a future."

Jeremiah 29:11

A HIGHER POWER

When right or wrong is at stake,
The law is supposed to decide, it's job, a decision to make.
But with the world filled with hate and crime,
Finding justice, sometimes, requires the law to work overtime.

At the end of the day, laws or not, God will decide,
Who's right or wrong, the ultimate moral guide.
Those in the know, will follow the Lord's lead,
Where legal and moral decisions, together intercede.

Our Lord God, may take matters in hand,
Silently punishing offenders, part of his redemptive plan.
Bringing love and faith, thereby altering the course,
Making true believers out of sinners, without using force.

It's God's way of improving mankind,
Guaranteeing the future, giving all people, peace of mind.
The highest power, greater than great,
We stand in awe, believing, awaiting our fate.

GOD

"I am the light of the world, whoever follows me will never walk in darkness, but will have the light of life."

John 8:12

THE LORD'S PLAN

At birth, all babies have the same chance,
God knows that some will lead, when they dance.
Some will follow, and others will just watch,
Those who resist will be left feeling hollow.

The Lord has a plan for each,
Revealed by Him, it's out of everyone's reach.
It's not in writing, or carved into a tree,
Not for purchase, but to all, it will be free.

It could be right before someone's eyes,
Not discovered, always a surprise.
It can come from within, in the dead of night,
Straight to the brain, though not through sight.

Like a great idea, that just pops into your head,
God's plan is clearly delivered as a dream, while you're in bed.
The only condition to learning your fate,
It is to accept Christ as your Savior, it's not smart to wait.

The potential to those that truly understand,
Is unlimited as to the faithful that follow the plan.
Those accepting the plan will be treated all with respect and care,
And the good in life for them, will be found everywhere.

GOD

"But you, man of God, flee from all this and pursue righteousness, godliness, faith, love, endurance and greatness."

1 Timothy 6:11

THE ROAD TO RIGHTEOUSNESS

Throughout history, God has tested man,
Sending the English Knights to fight Saladin and his caravan.
The plague brought by rats, that killed so many,
The world filled with hunger, there was no horn of plenty.

Religion brought slaughter, in the name of the Lord,
The non-righteous dispatched by the King's sword.
It was religion, that put the Pilgrims to sea,
To the new world, so they could worship openly and free.

Explorers always had God on their side,
Discovering new lands, while the natives would hide.
Wars and persecution, defined the path of progress,
Man's destiny, based on righteousness, all would confess.

History has recorded this real drama,
The downtrodden praying to survive, always suffering trauma.
The human race, always relying God,
Based on Righteous beliefs, and faith that's true and broad.

GOD

"Give, and it will be given to you. Good measure, pressed down, shaken together, running over will be put in your lap. For with the measure you use it, it will be measured back to you."

Luke 6:38

THE GIVER OF LIFE

There is only one, God, the giver of all,
We humbly worship Him, and His son, per religious protocol.
The wonder of His creations, all things on earth,
Defining each and every species, giving them worth.

All living creatures, integrated so well,
An ecosphere so unique, created for life to dwell.
His unbelievable attention to detail,
Every aspect perfect, all created in scale.

We all continue in awe of our Lord Almighty,
In reverence to the past, present, and what may be.
Our world, our home, just one planet of billions,
 Stretching across the universe, wide, light years in the millions.

So, to our one and only God, that has truly blessed us,
We Honor His gifts, a life-long plus.
Thankful to be uplifted by the Giver of Life,
A gift to all, whether a husband, child or wife.

FAITH AND REDEMPTION

"See what kind of love the Father has given to us, that we should be called children of God, and so we are. The reason why the world does not know is that it did not know him."

1 John 3:2

A CHILD OF GOD

In Jesus's flock, true believers indeed,
The Holy gospel, scripture for all Christians to heed.
Given the path to eternal life, morals a must,
Believing and righteousness, ideals to trust.

Being a "Child of God", connected to the Lord,
Avoidance of sin, temptation to avoid.
Not an easy task, in this wicked world,
Anger hate and racism, too many rocks hurled.

The challenge in life, to rise above it all,
Stay in the flock, follow God's call.
Not just a moniker, being one of God's own,
 Sinners have a debt to Christ, for all sins atoned.

Finding meaning and purpose, faith is the key,
The deliverance from evil, for some a wait and see.
On the day of judgment, rewards so great,
Believing is the ticket, for a "Child of God" to pass through Heaven's Gates.

FAITH AND REDEMPTION

"For the grace of God has appeared, bringing salvation to all men."

Titus 2:11

SALVATION

Jesus Christ, Our Savior, our Lord,
Giver of eternal life, He became so adored.
Being saved by Him, a blessed gift,
Truly for humanity, a millennial shift.

No longer fearing eternal death after earthly death,
Man's vision of eternity changed, forever with of His breath.
The concept of "Salvation", introduced by God,
Using His son as the lamb, His sacrifice has left us awed.

The Bible chronicling the events at that time,
The Disciples' witness, to Christ's wonder in his prime.
Miracles performed, just a glimpse of his power,
The story playing out, Christ, the man of the hour.

Worshippers become Christians, once they accept the Lord,
Christ's presence guaranteed, being with him, a perfect accord.
The gift of "Salvation", the world's ultimate prize,
Afterlife in heaven, an eternal surprise.

FAITH AND REDEMPTION

"But we did not receive the spirit of the world but the spirit, which is from God, that we know the things that have been given to us by the Grace of God."

1 Corinthians 2:12

BY THE GRACE OF GOD

When uncertainty looms, in times of need,
Those threatened, pray and take heed,
"By the Grace of God", their tearful cry,
Waiting to be saved, God standing by.

Centuries have passed, nothing has changed,
Atheists and Agnostics pronounced deranged.
It's pure faith, in God we put our trust,
 Our forefathers saying, "Believe in God", to survive we must.

Through hurricanes, tornadoes and volcanic eruptions,
Our faithful citizens have avoided disruptions.
Through this path of righteousness and belief,
 Our nation has prospered, always finding relief.

Now as we move forward, our future put in danger,
Let us not change course, into something stranger.
God is present with us each day,
Keeping vigilant and strong, to our God we pray.

Each day is a gift, to be used for the best,
Our children and descendants count on this quest.
Make the world a better place for everyone,
"By the Grace of God", we praise His only son.

FAITH AND REDEMPTION

"But by the Grace of God, I am what I am."

1 Corinthians 15:10

FINDING GRACE

Man is imperfect, it's human to sin,
Finding grace and forgiveness, takes humility and chagrin.
Asking Jesus to forgive and redeem,
Confessing your weakness, like a bad dream.

Facing the Lord, asking for a reprieve,
Wondering what penalties await, anxiety to relieve.
It's all part of the process of "Finding Grace",
Among Christian friends, a must to save face.

Admitting to sins and confessing at Jesus's request,
Having your sins forgiven true relief, when you're trying to be your best.
Life is a journey, not one day guaranteed,
Faith in the Lord, it's the only thing you need.

If you're troubled or depressed,
Seek the love of Jesus and forget being stressed.
There are many lifetime choices that you can be embrace,
Find faith in Jesus Christ and be rewarded with "Finding Grace".

FAITH AND REDEMPTION

"For God So Loved the World, that he gave   his only Son, that whoever believes in Him should not perish but have eternal life."

John 3:16

GETTING CLOSER TO GOD

Each day when you rise,
God presents a new day, a new sunrise.
The wonder of the world, so dynamic and great,
A new adventure, a new lesson for all, truly awaits.

The presence of the Lord, enhances each day,
With no fear or trepidation, it's easy to work and play.
Each step down the road, easier to take,
The joy of the experience, exciting to make.

Getting closer to God, comes from the soul,
Having inner feelings to connect, so as to set a life-long goal.
Being a true Christian, having undeniable faith,
Doing the Lord's work, without fear of his wraith.

Protected by the Lord, guaranteed eternal life,
Raising a family, helping others being a good husband or a wife.
The righteous path of family and faith are part of God's plan.
A special journey, for each woman and man.

Happiness and peace, are the rewards for being true,
The Grace of God available to all but availed by just a few.
So simple the commitment to righteousness and belief,
The resulting joy and peace provide a lifetime of relief.

FAITH AND REDEMPTION

"Now faith is the assurance of things hoped for, the conviction of things not seen."

Hebrews 11:1

NEVER WALK ALONE

In the walk of life, you're never walk alone,
Jesus is always present, your sins to atone.
He's with you, mind, body and spirit,
No fear, or worry, or demon can dispirit.

Belief a pre-requisite, for this special protection,
Nothing on earth will cause his defection.
Truth and justice are part of His plan,
Eternal life, for each woman and man.

Never think for a moment that He's not there,
Jesus Christ, the Son of God, is everywhere.
In church His presence is felt by all,
The Gospel as read, will cause all to stand tall.

At Communion, in remembrance of Him,
Bread and wine are served with a hymn.
It's the joy of never being alone,
Jesus waiting in Heaven, the date of your arrival is set,
For His grace and love to be shown.

FAITH AND REDEMPTION

"Therefore, if any man be in Christ, he is a new creature; old things are passed away; behold, all things become new."

2 Corinthians 5:17

A NEW LIFE IN CHRIST

Sometimes at the start of life it can be so full of trouble, so rocky,
Youthful mistakes, being arrogant and cocky.
Crime and drugs, maybe behind bars,
Remorse, depression, sad memoirs.

One trip to church, seeing the light,
Accepting Jesus Christ, a new life in sight.
Sins aplenty, now far behind,
A new lease on life, going from bad to kind.

Each day a miracle, great promise ahead,
Jesus ever present, no demons to dread.
Belief the igniter, the flame of faith now bright,
Salvation now a reality, Heaven in sight.

"A New Life", Christ's promise to each sinner,
So, uplifting, now feeling like a winner.
Just one step in the right direction,
Will change it all, accepting the Lord's gift of love and affection.

FAITH AND REDEMPTION

" Draw near to God and he will always draw near to you."

James 4:8

THANKFUL FOR CHRIST

The greatest thing to be thankful for,
Eternal life in Heaven, peace forevermore.
A gift from Jesus, paid for with his sacrifice,
Honoring Him, no one should think twice.

The Christian faith, so simple and pure,
Praising Christ, the King, the future guaranteed to endure.
No other religion, honors God's only son,
From heaven to earth, He's the only one.

In moments of meditation at communion,
Remembering the Lord is a spiritual reunion.
Bread and wine, offered to all,
It's a true homage to Jesus, religious protocol.

Giving thanks, a lifelong passion,
Praying to the Lord, an act of compassion.
The world is blessed, to have such a generous God,
On our knees we are and will remain totally awed.

HEALING THROUGH FAITH

"I press on toward the goal for the price of the upward call of God in Jesus Christ."

Philippians 3:14

IT'S GOD'S CALL

When a loved one passes comes inevitable grief,
The only solace, faith and belief.
Heaven, always said to be a better place,
Enjoyed by all who die, furnished by God's Grace.

The memories of a life gone, so precious and dear,
Grieving a serious process, sympathies given to hear.
Nothing can fill the void caused by death,
Life is so valuable; it is cherished with every breath.

Going on in one's life journey, is a true must,
Each person's time to pass is different, a promise from God's trust.
The lessons of life, taught each day,
Births, deaths, illness, and prayers to say.

The reality of living is faced by all,
No set time for it to end, it's God's call.
So, embrace each moment, if it were your last,
Time is running out for everyone, ever so fast.

HEALING THROUGH FAITH

" God is our refuge and strength, a very present help in times of trouble."

Psalm 46:1

IN TIMES OF TROUBLE

Finding solace, and peace of mind,
When things go wrong, when the world's unkind.
Just make a plan to move ahead,
Try to avoid the pitfalls and setbacks, that anyone might dread.

The best of plans, can still go awry,
Stress and worry, make you wonder why?
All the smarts often can't make things right,
It's a real paradox in life, there are no solutions, no one to call or write.

It's then that turning to God, and asking for help,
Can make more of a difference, than Google or Yelp.
Faith and prayer, the foundations of belief,
May bring a miracle, a chance for relief.

Over time, all things eventually work out,
Not always the way you wanted, but no reason to pout.
Just trust the Lord, to show you the way,
In one's life, it's always best to bring the Lord into play.

Meditation, reflection, finding your inner self,
A clear mind is not found in a jar on a shelf.
Look within, just take a deep breath,
The Lord is with you, in life and after death.

HEALING THROUGH FAITH

"I pray that all may go well with you and you may be in good health, as it goes with your soul."

3 John 1:2

HEALING THE WOUNDED SOUL

Losses in life, too many to count,
Stress, death, failure, emotional losses mount.
Finding an oasis, difficult to recover and heal,
Nearly impossible to find that place, so surreal.

Faith and devotion, needed to search for a resolution,
The path to recovery, prayer to Christ, for absolution.
The process complex and long, to be made whole,
Significant the time, to heal the wounded soul.

So impossible to understand how you got there,
Perhaps poor choices, dead ends, ending up in nowhere.
Life's conundrums, choosing the right fork in the road,
The result of a bad choice damaged by a ride with Mr. Toad.

All things considered, I'm lucky to be alive,
Five close calls, each time on a test drive.
What appears to be my new life goal,
Living with peace and joy, healing my wounded soul.

HEALING THROUGH FAITH

"I Then you will call on me and come and pray to me and I will listen to you."

Jerimiah 29:12

PRAYING FOR RELIEF

Often life is filled with misery and pain,
Daily struggles, that show no gain.
Praying for relief is the only choice,
Asking for a miracle, a moment to rejoice.

Modern medicine, often can't find a cure,
The only solution, a heavenly angel, relief to secure.
The trust needed to stay patient, during the wait,
Asking the Lord, over and over, no time to hesitate.

Just when you think the Lord isn't listening,
Relief comes, a new dawn, a belief re-christening.
Renewed faith, prayers answered after all,
The communication complete, a successful call.

The unity of a prayer chain, increasing the request,
All Christians together, inviting others to be a guest.
Placing yourself in the Hands of the Lord,
A gift from God, a reward all Christians can afford.

JESUS BY MY SIDE

"Teaching them to observe all that I have commanded you. And Behold I am with your always, to the end of the age."

Matthew 28:20

BEYOND MY CONTROL

Each day, when I rise,
The new day, so glorious, like a prize.
Making plans to get things done,
The Lord ever present, while I'm on the run.

Our busy lives, usually too much to do,
Always wondering how you always follow through.
So many details, and you're constantly there,
My words turn to actions, because of you, without a care.

As each day passes, my life in your hands, "Beyond my Control",
Through your guiding hand, lots of goodness, to extol.
Giving to those in need is your mission,
Invisible to all, seamlessly you act, without condition.

Words can't describe your power and wonder,
Your presence only seen in the sky, when there's lightning and thunder.
Oh, Glorious Lord, we stand in awe,
You are everything, ultimate judge, above the law.

JESUS BY MY SIDE

"But the Lord stood at my side and gave me strength."

2 Timothy 4:17

WITH THE LORD BY YOUR SIDE

Life's journey, so tenuous and sometimes brief,
Accidents, mishaps and disease, bringing pain and grief.
No miracles at hand, to make it right, so prayer is definitely needed,
To bring a calm and peace and fear is defeated.

When death brings grief, it's like a bad fall,
The anxiety and loss created, makes all of us feel small.
There is hope and love, for those that suffer, to get out of that place,
Freely given from above to those in need, through the Lord's grace.

Life's ups and downs, so hard to describe,
Remedies for relief so unique, no drugs available to prescribe.
Just when it seems that all is well,
The tide turns, and things go to hell.

The Lord has given each one of us strength,
Deep in our soul our will is tested at length,
The road of life is long and often it can be a bumpy ride,
A much better trip, with the Lord by your side.

JESUS BY MY SIDE

"Are not all angels ministering   spirits sent to those who will inherit salvation?"

Hebrews 1:14

SAVED BY AN ANGEL

Reckless and carefree are a dangerous pair,
Driving too fast, on a stupid dare.
Losing control of the car, wondered what was next,
My phone beeped; it was an anonymous text.

The phone speaker rang out, I turned the wheel right,
Reacting automatically, probably out of fright.
The car suddenly corrected, and stayed on the road,
 I stopped the car immediately and remained in recovery mode.

Looking at my phone, for the name of the unknown sender,
It said, "Angel Baby", the heavenly defender.
Shocked and stunned, I asked myself why,
A voice in my head said, "You're too young to die!"

Since that night, I've changed my ways,
Reading the Bible, giving the Lord praise.
There's no question, I would have died,
Saved by an angel, my heavenly guide.

JESUS BY MY SIDE

"Give all your worries and cares to God for

he cares about you."

Peter 5:7

JESUS AT THE WHEEL

There are times when faith is so important and danger is so real,
Lost on a strange road, death waits, with one wrong turn of the wheel.
No guard rails, a cliff just off the road,
White knuckles on the wheel, my fear definitely showed.

Praying to Jesus to help me out,
Alone and afraid, regarding my survival I had some serious doubt.
It was at that moment, I felt Jesus's hand,
Guiding my turns, He was the one in command.

No words can describe, the relief that I felt,
Like getting four aces, in every poker hand dealt.
As the car glided along that road so dark,
I felt angels hovering over me, but I heard no hark.

The car was not a self-driver, but Jesus definitely drove the car,
Being with Him that night, I felt like a superstar.
Never before or since, have I felt so good,
Believing in Christ saved me, something now so understood.

My experience of that night, could have turned out so wrong,
Jesus's presence enabled me to stay strong.
There is often no second chance, when death rears its head,
Making faith your armor, puts all dangers to bed.

HEAVEN

"But our citizenship is in heaven. And we eagerly await a Savior from there, the Lord Jesus Christ."

Philippians 3:20

A DAY IN HEAVEN

Near perfect weather every day,
God controlling the weather, holding the rain at bay.
Happiness abounds, Jesus's presence, the key,
Everything there, extra special and free.

No sickness, disease or pain,
No money or greed, no profit or gain.
The body now an intangible, the brain still the same,
Joy and happiness, a constant refrain.

Learning a new language, now takes a day,
Mastering the guitar easy, rock and roll, to play.
Dancing to music every day, joy to display,
Being yourself without fear, come what may.

The activity director is always the Lord,
His leadership so great, everyone in accord.
Games, competitions, all in fun,
A race for the marathoners, always on the run.

A perfect place, earned by all behind the pearly gates,
Enjoying God's paradise, everyone celebrates.
Each day is filled with grace and joy,
Amazing, fantastic, unbelievable,
It's Heaven for God's flock to enjoy.

TIME FOR PRAYER

"Then you will call on me and come and pray to me and I will listen."

Jeremiah 29:12

TIME FOR PRAYER

A loved one in peril, a life at risk,
Heart beats are faster, circulation brisk.
Wondering about the future, tears so near,
Surgery needed; emotions bring fear.

A time for prayer, asking for strength,
Needing the Lord's support, praying at length.
What is possible? What will be?
A serious time for concern, a wait and see.

It's at these moments, the Lord is near,
Holding our hearts, and worries understood, stresses to clear.
Pleading for a miracle, a healing result,
The Lord's help requested, a heavenly consult.

Never lose faith, the answer is Christ,
He's always there for us, confirming His sacrifice.
When times are dire, look above,
Healing, recovery and health brought by His love.

MEDITATIONS OF THE HEART

"May the words of my mouth and the meditations of my heart be pleasing in your sight, Lord my rock and redeemer."

Psalm 19:14

MEDITATIONS FROM THE HEART

The subject of faith, close to your heart,
Wondering about mortality, is a good place to start.
So personal in nature, difficult to discuss,
Counseling with your pastor is a real plus.

Understanding life's choices, the good and the bad,
Making poor decisions, definitely sad.
Looking inward, praying for blessings,
Thankful that sins are forgiven, after sincere confessions.

Church on Sunday, a weekly renewal of convictions,
Sorting out feelings, understanding contradictions.
Humble reflections, trying and complex,
Part of life's struggles, like understanding the opposite sex.

The meditations of the heart, contact with the Lord,
Praying to God, our creator, so adored.
Trusting your feeling, belief in the Word,
Understanding and believing, the Greatest Story ever heard.

THE SERMON

"Preach the word, be ready in season and out of season, reprove, rebuke and exhort with complete patience and teaching."

2 Timothy 4:2

THE SERMON

A message about Christ, in one half hour,
Filled with prayer, scripture, and parables with power.
Delivered by a Pastor, Priest or Layman,
 Always blessed as a part of God's holy Plan.

From Christmas, to Advent, then Easter, so dear,
Stories of Jesus's life, so uplifting to hear.
The wonder of Christ's words, now gospel to all,
 Written by Matthew, Mark, Luke, John and Paul.

Stories told of miracles, helping the needy and poor,
Bring his love and forgiveness, without grandeur.
Jesus so humble and pure, bringing us God's Grace,
Then ascending to Heaven, without a trace.

The sermon more than words, in every church,
A message of faith, from pulpit, floor or perch.
To each and every one, a reminder of Christ's sacrifice,
Eternal life in Heaven, committed belief the only price.

TO WORSHIP

"Oh come, let us worship and bow down; let us kneel before the Lord our Maker."

Psalm 95:12

WELCOME TO WORSHIP

At church for worship, most are so happy just to be there,
The Pastor, welcoming all, with open arms.
A religious message is needed to calm nerves from the world's false alarms.

As all rise, the opening hymn,
The message presented, worship, with vigor and vim.
It's the process of honoring, our Lord,
Church is the place, where He is adored.

The reverence and grace, available to all,
Just accepting Jesus as your Savior, answering his call.
The possibilities endless, arriving for the service,
Honoring Christ, no need to be nervous.

The warmth of the welcome, starting the day,
A prelude to the sermon of the day.
No better way to spend Sunday morn,
Attending church is a time to be reborn.

FINDING YOUR SOUL

"But if from there you seek the Lord your God, you will find him if you seek him with all your heart and soul."

Deuteronomy 4:29

FINDING YOUR SOUL

When the question of morality is addressed,
Civilized standards are used, most times, sins are confessed.
Always a battle between each person and his or her higher self,
Finding one's soul, the center of oneself.

Being a Christian is an essential component of the quest,
Finding love and compassion, equate to being blessed.
Mix in the husband or wife, kids, mom and dad,
Family, so precious, a life so happy, not sad.

This journey through life, a journey so natural and real,
God's plan for each one of us, seems so surreal.
The feeling of rising up, as you age, so fast it's meteoric,
Finding your soul, so important, it's much more euphoric.

Like a miracle, when it occurs, like straight from above,
Better than being knighted, having God's Love.
An audience with the Lord, absolutely guaranteed,
Guilt and sins are gone, lifted up, and your soul is set free.

Jubilation, exhilaration, and exaltation, words so dear,
Just human feelings, when God is near.
With His guidance, loving and living is yours to be,
Each day so precious, your soul is set free.

Author's Acknowledgements
•••

    The inspiration for this book of religious poems came from my faith in the Lord, and from support from my family, and friends. It has truly been an awakening experience to write poetry with religious and moral themes. In this time of uncertainty there is a real need to look to God for resolution of the chaos in the world. Finding answers to personal problems, health issues, loss of a loved one, catastrophic weather, or concern about the future, we need to look upward and pray for relief.

    I truly hope that the poems give you inspiration to look within and above and find a place for peace, joy and love.

    With the continued inspiration from my wife, Marylynn, my son, A.J., my sister-in-law, Sally Rygmyr, and my friends, Ralph and Susan Erickson, I have continued to write poems. I especially want to thank Amy Peterson and Diana Lang for their help in finding the perfect scripture for each one of the poems and reading and editing the poems.

    I give thanks for the opportunity to publish this second work of poetic religious verse.

JPK

•••

www.ingramcontent.com/pod-product-compliance
Lightning Source LLC
Chambersburg PA
CBHW051406290426
44108CB00015B/2171